All about God

A Basic English Resource for the Church

Adrian Reynolds

the knowledge
simple resources for the hungry church

Kerygma Resources
c/o Yateley Baptist Church
Cricket Hill
Yateley
Hampshire
GU46 6BA
United Kingdom

For more information visit the website www.theknowledge.org.uk

First published 2008 in English

A catalogue record for this book is available in the British Library.

ISBN 10   0-9541.5282-4
ISBN 13   978-0-9541-5282-6

Set in 11pt Bell MT.

Printed in the UK by thinkink, 11-13 Philip Road, Ipswich, Suffolk, IP2 8BH.
www.think-ink.co.uk

Index

This book is for Pathiyhar,
serving the Lord Jesus in Chandauli, India

Thank you to

Tom, who got me going
Isaac, who kept me going
Celia who allowed me to go
Eric, who kept me on the narrow road
Yateley Baptist Church who gave me time

May God bless you all!

Start here

This book is all about knowing God. That is what Christianity is about. It is written using the Simple English language with only 1,500 basic words. We hope that makes it easy to read. Sometimes Christians use words that are not simple. We will explain these words and write the Christian word as well. For example, we could say this book is all about knowing God [***theology***]. Then when others use these Christian words you will know what they mean. We often use verses from the Bible. To save space, these are not written out in full. You will find the Bible references written on the side of the page. Please look these up to make sure what we are writing is true.

An important question we must ask is this: how do we know what God is like? Men and women have different ideas about God. How do we know which ones are right? How do we know which ones are wrong? Christians believe that we can know what God is like in two ways.

First, we can look around us and see the world that God has made [Christians call this ***general revelation***]. What does this show us about God? It shows us that he is powerful. It takes great power to make mountains, seas, rivers, hills, trees, plants, animals and fish. When we look at the things God has made we see how powerful he is.

Romans 1:20

We can also see that God is not like us. God is not another man or woman. He is very different from us. We cannot make things like mountains or seas. Christians often use the word [***holy***] to describe this difference. We will think about this later on.

You can see that there are things we would like to know about God that we cannot tell by looking at what he has made. We cannot tell exactly what he is like. We cannot tell how it is possible to know God. We cannot tell why he has made the world and made men and women. To answer all these questions we need more detail from God. God has given us this detail in a book we call The Bible. The Bible is the second way we can know about God. It gives us much more detail about God than we could get from looking at what God has made. [Christians call this **special revelation**].

Later on in this book we will think about the Bible and why we know we can believe what we read in it. For now, we will use the Bible to tell us more about God – what he is like and how we can know him.

What is God like?

God is different

The most important questions in life are: What is God like? How can we know him? This part of the book is all about what God is like. We have already said that God is different. He is not like us. This is a very good way to describe God. Christians use the word [*holy*] to describe this difference. Sometimes the word holy means never doing anything wrong. However, its true meaning is being different. For example:

- We are one person, God is three persons in one being;
- We begin as babies, grow up and die. God is different because he always lives and never dies;
- We often do things that are not right. God always does the right thing;
- We are limited in what we can do. God can do anything he pleases;
- We can only be in one place at a time. God is everywhere.

So, you can see that different [*holy*] is a great way to describe God. In the Bible, the angels call God "holy, holy, holy." In Hebrew – the language of the Old Testament – saying a word three times is a way of showing how true it is. So, the Bible teaches us that God is completely different from us and anything else we can see around us. All other ways of talking about God are part of this difference.

Isaiah 6:3

We would expect God to be different to all other things we know. If this were not so then he would not be God. He would just be another man or another animal. So, if we had to choose one word to describe God, this is the word we would use. Let's think of some of the other ways in which God is different.

God is three persons in one

We are one person. Sometimes we may have different feelings, but they all come from inside the one person. One of the most important **Deut. 6:4** ways that God is different from us is that he is three persons. This does not mean that God is three different beings. Time and time again, the Bible calls God One. But as One being, God is also the Father, the Son and the Holy Spirit – all at the same time.

This is, of course, very difficult to understand. We should not be surprised that understanding God is difficult – it is all part of him being different to us. In fact, the Bible does not try to explain how God can be three persons in one. Instead, it simply shows us it is true.

Genesis 1:26 How do we know God is more than one person even though **Isaiah 52:13** he is one being? Sometimes God uses the words "we" or "our" to describe himself. The Old Testament (the first part of the Bible) also **Exodus 31:3** uses very different words (such as "the King" or "the Servant" or "the Spirit of God") to refer to God.

In the New Testament, this becomes clearer. There are several parts of the Bible which refer to all three persons of God **2 Cor 13:14** together. Christians call this [*the Trinity*] though this is not a word that comes from the Bible.

As it is hard to understand, we may think that it does not matter if we believe this or not. However, it is very important for everything else we know about God to get this part right. For example, later on we will say that God has always been loving. But **John 17:24** God cannot be loving if he is not Three-in-One. Before the world was made, whom did he love? How did he know how to love? The answer is that he loved himself. The Father loved the Son, the Son loved the Spirit, the Spirit loved the Father and so on. It is only because God is Three-in-One that he can also be loving.

The Bible shows us clearly that the three persons are all fully God. The Father is God. The Son is God. The Holy Spirit is God. Yet God is also one being. So God is One and God is also Three. We often describe this using the words "Three-in-One."

Galatians 1:1
Colossians 2:9
John 15:26

The three persons of God do different things. For example, only Jesus the Son came to die on the cross. The Holy Spirit lives in Christians. But there are also things that all three do. The Bible teaches that the Father, the Son and the Holy Spirit all took part in making Jesus come back to life after he was killed.

Acts 2:24
John 10:18
Romans 1:4

We need to be careful that when we talk about "God" we know what we mean. Sometimes, in the Bible, God is used instead of "Father." This is often the case in the New Testament. At other times "God" means Father, Son and Holy Spirit all working together. This is often the case in the Old Testament. The word "LORD" written in the Bible in small capitals refers to the Jewish name YAHWEH which Christians believe is God the Three-in-One: Father, Son and Holy Spirit.

Acts 2:24

Psalm 1:6

This is one of the most important things we can know about God. It shows us that the God of Christianity is not the same as the gods in other religions. Hinduism, Islam and so on worship different gods, not the Three-in-One true God.

God is loving

Because God is three persons he is also loving. The three persons exist with one another. For example, when Jesus the Son was on earth he talked to the Father. In the Bible, we see the love that the three persons of God have for one another. God shows this love to the whole world in two ways.

Mark 1:35

Mark 1:11

Even though men and women don't love God, he still loves them. He would be right to be angry with men and women who don't love him, but he still makes the world turn and keeps the food growing. There was one time when God sent rain to cover the whole earth (in the time of Noah), but God has said he will never do this again.

Because this is more than men and women should get from God we call it grace. Grace means getting something that we should not get. Christians call this love [**common grace**] because God shows it to all men and women.

This love or common grace does not mean that everything always goes right for everybody. Clearly, it does not. It simply means that God's love can be seen in the way in which he keeps the world going.

The second way God shows his love is by making some men and women his children. We still call this love grace because, as we shall see later, we should be turned away by God – instead he makes us part of his family. Christians call this kind of love [**saving grace**].

This is the main way God loves us. It is not the only way, but it is the most important because if there were no saving grace then we could not be God's children. A well known verse in the Bible is John 3:16. This shows us that God's love is firstly about saving grace.

God wants to talk to us

Part of God's love is that he wants us know him and love him. You cannot love someone that you never talk to. God wants us to talk to him – we call this prayer. He also wants to talk to us. He does this through the Bible which we sometimes call God's Word. This is such an important thing to learn that we will come back to it in another part of the book (How does God speak to us?).

God has always existed

Another way that God is different from us is that he has always existed [he is **eternal**]. Even before he made the world God was there. There was never a moment when God (Father, Son and Holy Spirit) was not living. There will never be a moment when he is not living. Our lives are ruled by time. Our days last 24 hours. An hour has 60 minutes and so on. God is outside time, because time comes from the way the earth turns and God existed before he made the earth. However far back you could go, you would always find God living. How ever far forward you could go, you would always find God living. Psalm 90:2

All of us start off as babies. We grow and develop. Then, at some point, we will die. This is the same for every man and woman. It is never true for God [he is **immortal**]. 1 Timothy 1:17

God never changes

Because God has always been there, it should not surprise us that God never changes [he is **immutable**]. He has always been the same, and will always be the same. Men and women change a lot. We change in the way we look and the way we think. We do not think the same way as grown ups as we do when we are children. We learn and develop. Malachi 3:6 James 1:17 Hebrews 13:8

However, God is always the same. This also means that he does not change the way he is. All these things we are learning about God will always be true. The things we read about God in the Bible will always be true, even though they were written down a long time ago. God also never changes his mind. We can depend on God being the same whatever may happen to us.

God is without limits

Isaiah 55:8-9 We have already seen that God is without limits when it comes to time. He has no start and no end. In fact every part of him is without limits. He is as far above us as it is possible to be [he is **transcendent**]. The Bible says this is true for God's thoughts, ways, and love as well as other parts of his character. This is another way to think about God. It is also the reason why we should worship him.

God always does the right thing

Deut 32:4 Another important thing to understand about God is that he always does the right thing [he is **righteous**]. In fact, we can go further than this and say he loves the right thing to be done. The Bible shows us this using different words. One of the main words we use is justice. As God always does the right thing, this means that God is always just (sometimes we say that God is the Judge).

Of course, we sometimes don't understand why God does some things. But just because we don't understand them does not mean that God is wrong. It is more likely that our minds are not able to see what God is doing.

It is great to know that God is right and just. This means that every person who does things wrong will have to answer to God. They do not always have to do so right away, but the Bible shows us that there will be a day when God calls men and women to suffer **Romans 14:12** the punishment for whatever they have done [**the Day of Judgement**].

Again this shows how different we are to God. None of us always does the right thing. Sometimes we do, sometimes we don't — but no one *always* does the right thing. This is why we cannot know God unless God does something about the fact that we are not always right. We will talk about this in another part of the book.

8

God is able to do anything

God has no limits when it comes to what he can do [he is **omnipotent**]. This is another way that he is different from us. Nothing is difficult for God. This is great news for Christians who face hard times. God can do anything. If he does not do something we ask, it is not because he cannot but because he will not – he has another, better plan. It is this power that gives Christians great help through the whole of life.

Luke 1:37
Romans 1:20

One of the most powerful things God can do is to make us his children. The Bible shows us that all of us were dead before we came to God. Only God had the power to make us living and part of his family. We could not do this ourselves, but God's power made it possible.

Ephesians 2:1

God exists everywhere

Yet another difference is that God is not limited to being in one place at a time. He exists everywhere [he is **omnipresent**]. There is nowhere on earth, or anywhere in the Universe where God does not exist. This means, of course, that we can never keep things from God. But it also means that wherever we go, God is there as well.

Psalm 139:8

God can be everywhere because he is a spirit. Jesus, the Son of God took on the form of a man when he came to earth, and he still keeps this form. Yet, God the Three-in-One is also spirit and so can be everywhere at the same time.

John 4:24

God knows everything

Because God is everywhere, he knows everything [he is **omniscient**]. He not only sees the things we do, but even the thoughts that are in our heads and what is in our hearts. This knowledge does not just mean that God sees things as they happen. Because God is

Psalm 139:1-4

outside time, he sees things before they happen. He knows the past, the present and the future.

God rules over all things

When we start to put the things we have learned together, we begin to see what God does. If God is powerful, knows everything and is everywhere then it must follow that he rules over all things [he is *sovereign*]. Nothing takes place without God knowing about it, or even allowing it to happen. He knows the future and he rules over all things to make them turn out as he wants [*providence*].

Of course, this is difficult to understand when it comes to evil things. Is it still true that God is ruling when we see or hear about bad things taking place? Yes, it must still be true because God does not change. And in some way, these bad things must be taking place for good reasons, because he is loving and always does the right thing.

Psalm 57:2 **Romans 8:28**

We have to believe the Bible when it shows us that God rules over all things. If he does not rule over all things, then he is not powerful. If he is not powerful, then he is not God. The only explanation when bad things happen is that God does know what he is doing.

Millions of Christians find this a great help. We all face difficult times. Sometimes the bad things are very close to us indeed. But God is always ruling over the Universe, and as one Bible man (Abraham) says, the Judge of all the world will always do the right thing.

Genesis 18:25

God made the world

The last thing we shall learn about God is that he made everything [he is *omnific*]. This is so important that we shall look at it in the

Genesis 1

next part of the book. The Bible tells us that God made the world from nothing. Before the world existed only God existed. He made all that we see around us out of nothing. He did it by speaking. Because he is powerful his voice is enough to make the world, the planets, the stars and everything else we can see.

Of course, the Bible shows us much more about God than these basic things. But these are a great place to start. Because God is so far above us, we will never be able to fully understand him [we are *finite*, he is *infinite*]. This is why growing as a Christian is never complete. Even in heaven, there will always be something more to know about God.

What should we do once we have seen all these things about God? The Bible says we should praise God. This means we should say how great he is and say that he alone is Lord and God. **Nehemiah 9:6**

11

What has God made?

God made all things

We must now think about what God has made. Why is this an important thing to think about? We said that the two most important questions are What is God like? and How can we know him? We have started to answer the first question. To answer the second question we have to see how men and women came into the world. This means we have to think about what God has made [*creation*].

Nehemiah 9:6 The Bible teaches us that God made all things. Nothing exists that God has not made. This is true for all the things we see around us: rocks, mountains, rivers and seas. God did not just make the world as we know it. He also made the entire Universe. The Universe is very big – no one can measure it. But we know it has a great number of stars and that it goes on for a very long way. This is all part of what God has made. God made all these things in the past.

But God also continues to make things now, though it is not quite the same. For example, we may know from science why certain things happen. We may be able to explain why a seed **Psalm 104:14** planted in the earth grows into a crop of grain, but it is still God making it happen. God is still making things.

This is because God is ruling over all things, as we have already seen. So, for example, it is true to say that God made the first man, Adam, and the first woman, Eve. We shall think about **Psalm 139:13** them in a moment. But even though we might understand how babies are made in great detail, it is still true that every one is made by God.

Psalm 24:1 Because God made all things, the Bible shows us that all things belong to God as well. How did God make the Universe we see around us?

12

God started with nothing

We learned in the last part of the book that God has always existed. This is what makes him different from everything else around us. So there was a time when only God existed, as everything else must have a start. This means that when God made things, he made them from nothing. This seems very hard to us. When we make things, we always have to start with something. For example, when we make food to eat, we have to start with basic things, like water or meat.

Genesis 1:1

When God made the world he started with nothing. The Bible does not use these actual words to describe what God has made, but the idea is clearly taught. It is important because it shows that God is different from us and that he is very powerful.

Hebrews 11:3

Father, Son and Holy Spirit made all things

We learned that God is Three-in-One. Who made the world? Was it God the Father, or God the Son, or God the Holy Spirit? The Bible teaches us that all three were part of the work of making the world. This is helpful to us when we try to see what God is like. Before anything else was made, only God existed and he has always been Three-in-One. That is why all three persons work to make the world. For example, we read that the world was made by the Father, through Jesus and that the Spirit of God was there right at the start.

**1 Cor 8:6
John 1:3
Genesis 1:2**

All things were made for God

Why did God make the world? We might like to think that he made it for us – a good place to live and grow. In fact, God made the world for himself, first of all. He made it to show how great he is. Even today, when the world is not as it should be, this is still true.

Psalm 19:1-2

We can be more clear about this, because the Bible shows us that all things were made for Jesus. It is always good to remember that this is what everything God has made is for. Even men and women are made for Jesus, to bring praise and honour to his name.

This is our purpose and the purpose of the entire Universe.

How did God make things?

We have learned that the Father, Son and Holy Spirit were all part of making everything we see. But if God made the world from nothing, how did he do it? The Bible shows us time and time again

that God did it by his words. He said the words and it took place.

This is hard for us to understand as we cannot do anything like this. However, remember that God is able to do all things, so even making things by using words is not hard for him.

When Jesus, God's Son, came to earth he also used words to make things happen. For example, he used words to make men and

women better when they were ill. This shows us that God's words are powerful enough to make the world. In the Bible, Jesus is given the name The Word, because of his powerful voice that makes

things happen.

The days of making

The Bible shows us that the world was made by God in a certain order. There are six days of making and God makes different things on different days. You can read about these on the first page of the Bible. The six days are made up of two groups of three days which follow the same pattern.

Day 1: Day & Night   Day 4: Sun, moon and stars

Day 2: Sky & Water   Day 5: Birds & Fish

Day 3: Land & Plants   Day 6: Animals, men and women

14

Can you see the pattern? The first group of days match up with the second group of days. This order is part of the way that God makes all things. There are some things that are the same about all of these days.

The day starts with God's words. Then God's words come true. Then God sees that what he has made is "good." The only difference is on the last day when God sees that what he has made is "very good."

Science and the Bible

Some men and women of science believe that the world was made differently from the way God shows us in the Bible. It is important for us to see that the Bible does not say it is a science book. Sometimes hard things are explained using simple language so that we can understand them better. But even when the Bible does this it always shows the truth.

For example, a day could be 24 hours long or it could be much longer. God could be using a picture to show simple men and women like us how he made the world. He uses simple language like this in other parts of the Bible. The Bible does not try to show us every detail of how God made the world. It simply shows us that God made the world in a certain order using the power of his voice.

We do not need to worry that some men and women of science say that science shows us that God does not exist or that he did not make the world because God gives us faith to believe what the Bible says.

Hebrews 11:3

The seventh day

A week has seven days. God made everything in six days. On the seventh day he rested. This does not mean that he did nothing. It means that he rested from his work of making the Universe. He is

Genesis 2:2-3
Hebrews 1:3

15

still working to keep the world and Universe going [Christians say God is **sustaining** all things]. For God, this seventh day lasts until he makes everything new when Jesus comes to the earth again (we shall learn about this later in the book).

The seventh day is important because it gives us a work pattern to follow. Just as God worked for six days and then rested, so we should have a day of rest. In some countries with Christian laws, this is often Sunday, a day when Christians can meet together. It does not matter if we live in countries where the rest day is different, as long we follow this pattern.

God made angels

God made all things. This means God made the things we can see such as flowers, plants, animals, stars and so on. But he also made things we cannot see. This means that God made angels. The first page of the Bible does not tell us about angels, but other parts of the Bible show us that God made angels as well. They must have been made on one of the six days when God made everything.

Psalm 148:2-5

What are angels? In some ways, they are the same as men and women. Angels are made by God, just like men and women. We must not bow down before them, because God has made them, just as he has made us. In other ways, they are different from us. They do not have bodies and bones like we do. They have great power, though not as much as God.

The Bible shows us all about angels. We do not need to know everything about them right now, but it is important to understand that God made them. One particular angel plays a very important part once God has made men and women. His name is Satan (he is also called the Devil). This angel turned his back on God right from the start.

Luke 10:18

He took with him other angels [now called **demons**] and together they are against God and Christians and try to destroy every work of God.

God made men and women

The Bible shows us that God made men and women on Day number six. There is one very important difference about men and women. God makes them to be like him. He does not do this for any other thing he makes – even angels.

Genesis 1:26

What does it mean to be made like God? God is still different from us. However, there are things about us that make us like God, not like animals. If we looked back at the first part of this book we could use some of the ways we talked about God to talk about men and women as well.

For example, God likes to speak with us. God has made us to speak with him and with one another. As men and women it is good for us to be with other men and women, because that is how God has made us. This is why being a man and wife is very important. God made us to be go together. In fact, when a man and a wife have sex together and two become one, it is a strong picture of how God can be one and three at the same time.

Genesis 2:24

God always does the right thing. We do not always do the right thing, but God has given us the ability to understand right and wrong (unlike animals, for example). God rules over all things, and he gave the first man (called Adam) and the first woman (called Eve) the command to rule over the world.

Genesis 1:28

God did not give this command to any other thing he made, showing us that men and women have a very important part in God's plan. The rest of the Bible shows us how God wants men and women to know him.

Men and women turned away from God

Just like the angels, men and women turned away from God. This took place right from the start when Adam and Eve broke the one rule that God gave them. He gave them a rule not to eat from one tree in the garden he had made. This should have been a simple command to keep.

Genesis 3:1-7 The Bible shows us how Satan (the angel who had turned away from God) helped Eve to break God's rule. Then Eve helped Adam do it as well. This meant that Adam and Eve had not kept God's one command. God was in command, but Adam and Even turned away from God's command and made the rules they liked. We call this [*sin*] and it is such an important Bible word that we will use it from now on.

Sin came into the world

Sin is when men and women make the rules they want instead of taking God's rules. They make themselves king instead of making God the King. It started with Adam and Eve and it changed the world that God had made. When God first made everything he saw that it was very good.

Genesis 3:23 After Adam and Eve sinned the whole world was changed. Let us think about some of the important changes. The most important change is that Adam and Eve had to leave the garden that God had made for them and where he lived with them. They could not be with him in the same way. This is because of what God is like. Remember, that God always does the right thing and he is just. He cannot be with men and women who are not like him. Once Adam and Eve sinned, they had to leave God's garden. God made them to know him. Now their sin meant they could not know him. This is the first part of their punishment.

18

When God made Adam and Eve they would have lived for ever. Once they sinned, God made sure they would die. This was another part of the punishment for their sin.

Genesis 1:19

Instead of ruling over the world, God said that Adam would find it very difficult to grow food to eat. Although God still gave enough for him to eat, Adam had to work very hard in the fields.

Genesis 1:17-18

Eve would find it painful to have children. Before she sinned, having a baby would have been very easy. This is part of Eve's punishment for sin.

Genesis 1:16

God made Adam the perfect head of the family. Because he was made like God, he would be loving and kind. God told Eve that after she had sinned, Adam would not be so kind and loving in his rule over her. He also told Eve that she would want Adam's place as head. This is all part of the punishment for sin.

Genesis 1:16

You can see that these punishments continue today. Even when they do not know it, all men and women are separated from God. God is still the same. Men and women who do things wrong cannot know him. All men and women die. All men and women find it hard to grow food. All women have pain giving birth to children. Men are often hard in their family rule. Women often want to be like the man ruling the family.

Why do these punishments continue if Adam and Eve died thousands of years ago? It is because sin came into the world through Adam and Eve and it is still here.

All babies are full of sin

The Bible teaches us that even very young babies are full of sin. In fact, even as we grow inside our mothers we are still sinners. Sin is not just doing things wrong, but making ourselves kings, rather than living under God our King. We are sinners because we take on the sin of Adam, just like we take on other things from our mothers

Psalm 51:5

Romans 5:18 and fathers. Adam and Eve's sin is passed on from generation to generation and is a problem for all human beings [*original sin*].

Genesis 6-8 You can see that things do not look good for men and women. We can see this clearly because early on in the Bible God takes action against men and women who have turned away from him. He saves one man and his family, a man called Noah. Every other man and woman is killed by God in a flood because they have turned away from him. This is the same death we ought to have because we have sinned against God as well.

Genesis 3:15 Yet, when God makes Adam and Eve leave the garden he shows them Satan will one day be crushed by a man. God has a plan to sort things out and make it possible for men and women to know him after all. It is that man and that plan that we shall learn about now.

How can we know God?

The problem of sin

We have seen what God is like and what he has made. We turn now to the question of how men and women can know God. The sin of Adam and Eve is passed on to all men and women. This sin stops us from being able to know God. But we saw that God had a plan to sort things out and make it possible for us to know him. We saw how this plan was for a man to crush Satan, God's enemy. The man is Jesus.

Romans 5:12

We have already said that Jesus is God. God is three persons, Father, Son (Jesus) and Holy Spirit. How can Jesus be man and God at the same time? This important question helps us to understand what Jesus has done to make it possible for us to know God. Let us think about what the Bible teaches us about Jesus.

Jesus is fully man

When we read the Bible, we see that Jesus became a man. He was not always a man, but he became a baby, grew into a child and then into a man [the *incarnation*]. The four accounts of Jesus' life [the *Gospels*] written by Matthew, Mark, Luke and John are very clear that Jesus is fully man. You can read these to see some of the proof. Let us think about a few examples.

John 1

- Jesus started on the earth as a baby and grew as a normal child – just like us;
- Jesus got tired and needed food – just like us;
- Jesus felt pain – just like us;
- Jesus had feelings such as joy, sorrow and love – just like us;
- Jesus could die – just like us.

Luke 2:40
John 4:6
Matthew 21:18
Luke 10:21
Luke 23:46

These are just some of the things that show Jesus was fully man. We shall think a little later about why it was important that Jesus was fully man.

Some men and women claim that Jesus never lived. They say the Bible is not showing the truth when it shows us Jesus in this way and Christians have invented the stories about Jesus. But even books other than the Bible speak about Jesus. For example, some letters from the Roman Empire showed that Jesus lived and was killed by the Romans.

Jesus is fully God

Romans 9:5
John 1:1-2
Titus 2:13

Jews and Muslims also believe that Jesus was a man. But Christians believe something else about Jesus. Christians believe Jesus is fully God. The Bible makes it clear that this is true. There are several parts of the Bible which speak about Jesus being God. Please look them up.

John 10:14
John 8:58-59

Some men and women claim that Jesus himself never claimed to be God. However, he used some of the names of God for himself (like Shepherd, King, I AM and Lord) and the Jews knew he claimed to be God because they tried to kill him for it.

In the first part of this book we thought about what God is like. As Jesus is fully God, he is all of these things as well. He always does the right thing; he is different; he is loving; he is just; he knows all things; he can do all things; and so on.

Jesus is man and God at the same time

Christians believe that Jesus is man and God at the same time. When Jesus came to Earth he did not give up on being God. He was still God. After Jesus had come back to life and gone into heaven, he did not give up on being a man. He is still a man.

It is very important for Christianity that Jesus is man and God at the same time.

Because Jesus became a man he could live on Earth and deal with the problem of sin that Adam and Eve had made. We shall see how he did this in just a moment.

Because Jesus is God he did not take on the problem of sin that we get from our mothers and fathers. The Bible says that Jesus is like us in every way except without sin.

Hebrews 4:15

But how could this be possible? Was Jesus two persons? No! Jesus was and is one person. But just as it is possible for God to be three-in-one, even though we cannot understand it, it is also possible for Jesus to be man and God at the same time. Even though we cannot understand it, with God's help we can believe it is true.

1 Cor. 12:3

The birth of Jesus gives us more proof that this is the case. Jesus' mother was Mary. She was not married and had not had sex with a man. Jesus' father was not Joseph, as men and women thought. The baby was made in Mary by the power of the Holy Spirit [the **virgin birth**].

Luke 1:26-38

Some men and women ask, if Jesus is fully God, why did he sometimes say he did not know things, or why did he grow in wisdom, as the Bible says? That is a good question. We believe that the man side of Jesus [his **human nature**] grew and developed just like us, but that his God side [his **divine nature**] was always God.

Luke 2:52

This also helps us explain how Jesus could die. Although man can die, God cannot die – he lives forever. How could Jesus be killed? It was his man side that died when we was killed.

What did Jesus come to Earth to do?

Now we understand that Jesus came to Earth and was fully man and God at the same time. Why did he have to come to Earth? To understand the answer to this question, we have to understand a very important Bible idea. When someone does something wrong to someone else, that other person is often angry.

This is the way God feels about sin. Remember, he is different from us. He always does the right thing, and when men and women do not do the right thing they turn they back on him. Like Adam and Eve, he is not able to live with them and they are not able to know him. In fact, God is angry with them because of their sin [this is God's **wrath**].

Romans 1:18
Ephesians 2:3

Because God is just, there must be punishment for this sin. God cannot simply say "it does not matter" because sin always matters to him. Therefore, if sin exists, men and women cannot know God. The only way that God can be at one with us is if someone else comes and takes our sin away from us [**forgiveness**].

Who can do this? No other man or woman can take our sin away from us, because they have sin as well. We need someone who is like us (a man) but not like us, someone without sin. Can you see who this is? It is Jesus.

Hebrews 2:17

Only Jesus is able to take our sin upon himself. But this is only part of the work he came to do. Remember that God is always right and loves other men and women to be always right like him. Jesus takes our sin away, but he also gives to us his obedient life which he lived by always doing right [**justification**].

2 Cor 5:21

We sometimes say Jesus is our substitute. He took our sin away and gave us his life of obedience.

How did Jesus do this?

How did Jesus do all this? Could he not have just said the words? After all, he made the world with his words, so why could he not just take away our sins with words as well? Remember that God is just. In a court case, it would not be just if someone who has done something wrong is let off without a punishment. That would not be fair. We would be very cross about that. Because sin is turning away from God's rule, sin must also have a punishment. It would not be fair if God simply said "there is no punishment."

So, in order for our sin to be taken away and for us to receive Jesus' right life, God must give someone our punishment. Christians believe that Jesus was killed on a cross. Although this was arranged by the Jews and the Romans, the Bible shows us that this was part of God's plan. When Jesus was killed on the cross, he was taking God's punishment for our sin [Christians call this the atonement]. It is because Jesus died that we can be one with God again [reconciliation], just as Adam and Eve were when God first made them.

Acts 2:23

Romans 5:6

Colossians 2:11

This is why the cross is so important to Christians. When Jesus came to Earth he showed that he was always right by the way he lived. By doing this he gave us an example. He also gave good teaching and made ill men and women better. But this is not the main reason he came to Earth. Jesus himself said that he came to die for men and women.

Mark 10:45

Why did Jesus have to die?

Why did God the Father send Jesus his Son? Why did he not just leave men and women to die? He would be right to do this. It would be what men and women deserve. But he sent Jesus to die in our place. Why did he send Jesus? The answer is because of God's love.

1 John 4:10

25

Remember that we have already learned about saving grace. The cross is where love and justice meet together.

What took place after Jesus was killed?

If Jesus had just been a man, then his death would have been the end. For all men and women live then die. But, as we have learned, Jesus was not just a man. He was also fully God at the same time. So we would not expect death to be the end for him. Also, remember that one of the punishments Adam and Eve got from God was to die. If Jesus' death on the cross took away the effect of their sin, then we would expect something to happen after Jesus was killed. We would expect to see that Adam and Eve's punishment was no longer in place.

Mark 10:34   When Jesus was on the Earth, he taught his friends that three days after he was killed he would come back to life. Jesus was killed **Mark 16:17** on a Friday and when, on Sunday, some of his friends went to the place where his body had been left they found that he was not there.

Some men and women say that Jesus' body had been taken by thieves. However, there were Roman men guarding the place, so **Matthew 27:62-65** this could not have had taken place. Jesus had come back to life [the *resurrection*].

John 21:12 Jesus did not come back as a spirit. He came back to life as a man. He could eat and his friends could touch and feel his body. When Jesus came back to life he showed us that God was pleased with his death – it had done what he wanted it to do. It also showed us that even when we die, there is hope for us. One day, Jesus will bring all men and women back to life, just as he came back to life. **Romans 6:23** We can live forever, just as he does [*eternal life*]. Jesus has showed us that this is possible.

Is Jesus still on the Earth today?

If Jesus came back to life and can never die, where is he now? About 40 days after Jesus came back to life, the Bible shows us that Jesus went back to heaven, from where he came. Heaven is the place where God lives. In heaven, Jesus continues to rule over the world, just as he always has done.

However, Jesus does not leave men and women alone on the Earth. When Jesus was on Earth he could only be in one place at a time because he was fully man – just like us. But now he is in heaven he has sent his Holy Spirit to the Earth. Because the Holy Spirit is not a man, he is everywhere at the same time. Jesus said that this would be even better that having Jesus on Earth. The Holy Spirit continues the work that Jesus started. His work is so important that we shall learn about it in another part of this book.

John 14:12

How does the Bible describe Jesus' work?

Christians often think about the work of Jesus in three ways. These are ways the Bible uses to describe the work and help us understand what Jesus does [the **offices of Christ**]. In the Old Testament, we see that God talks about Jesus before he comes to Earth [**prophecies**]. In the New Testament, we see that what the Bible says about Jesus comes true [the prophecies are **fulfilled**].

First, Jesus is shown to be the one through whom God speaks [He is the **Prophet**]. Men who spoke God's words were known as [**prophets**]. One of God's greatest prophets, Moses, looks forward to a time when a great prophet would come. We have already seen how Jesus is called "The Word of God" and that his words are powerful, making all things. A prophet showed men and women what God thought and what God was like. Because Jesus is God himself, he is the best way we can know what God is like.

Deut. 18:15
Hebrews 1:1

27

Second, Jesus is called a Priest. In fact, he is called the Great High Priest. In the Old Testament, the priest was the man who came between God and men. He was the go-between [the *mediator*]. The priests offered prayer and praise to God for men and women, because men and women were sinful and so could not come near God. They killed animals [*sacrifices*] to show men and women how serious sin was.

Hebrews
10:1-3
These dead animals could not take away sin, but showed that the death of a right man could take away sin. In this way, they

Hebrews
7:26-28
pointed to Jesus. Unlike the priests who killed animals, Jesus let himself be killed to bring men and women to God.

The Bible shows us that the death of Jesus makes the way to God open because Jesus speaks up for us to his Father [we call this

Romans
8:34
Jesus *interceding* for us].

Revelation
19:16
Third, Jesus is called the King. A king rules over countries and men and women. The Jews of the Old Testament were looking forward to a king that God had said would come. They called this king the Messiah which means one who is covered with oil because he is king. This is a Hebrew name (the language that Jews spoke). In Greek (the language of the New Testament) it is Christ. It means the same thing. So, when we say Jesus Christ, we mean King Jesus.

John
18:36
The kingdom of Jesus is not like the kingdoms of this world. Jesus is not interested in countries and wars and land. He is interested in men and women making him King of their lives. A King is given authority to rule over his nation.

We can see even more clearly that we should bow down before Jesus and praise him for all that he is and all that he has done. However, we still have an important question to ask. How do the things that Jesus has done for us come to us now? We can see that Jesus has made it possible for us to know God. But how does it happen?

28

How does God save us?

Christians talk about being saved [**salvation**]. We have already learned what God saves us from. He saves us from sin and the punishment we should have. The Bible speaks about this punishment lasting forever. Remember that even though our bodies grow old and die, there is a part of us that lives for ever [the part we call our **soul**].

Romans 5:9

When our bodies die, our souls live on. Because of sin, these souls cannot be with God, so instead they are sent away from him for punishment. The place where souls are punished is called hell. Hell is not a good place. Jesus himself speaks about hell as a place of punishment, crying and weeping.

Mark 9:42-48

This is what we need to be saved from. We have already seen that Jesus saves by being killed on the cross. Our sin is taken from us and given to him. He takes our punishment. His right life is taken from him and given to us. We receive his good life.

But how does this happen? When does this take place?

The process must start with God. Remember, because of sin we are separated from God. In fact, we are already dead. Our bodies are not dead of course. They are living. But the inner part of us that lives for ever is dead with respect to God. We cannot come to him. We cannot know him. That puts us in a very bad position. We know we need to be made living again. But how? Dead men and women cannot bring themselves back to life.

Ephesians 2:1

The Bible shows us that God gives us life. He makes the first step. This is good news for us, as we were unable to take the first step. There are different words the Bible uses to describe this change. Jesus said it is being "born again" or "born from above" [**conversion**].

Ephesians 2:4

John 3:3

When did God decide to make this change in us? The answer is surprising. God made the decision to change us before he even made the world. This may sound strange, but remember, God knows the future, so even before he made the world, he planned how things would turn out. It was then he chose us [*election*] to be

Ephesians 1:4 saved.

If you are a Christian, it is because God chose you. You may think you chose him. Perhaps you can remember the moment when you said "Lord Jesus, I believe you took my place on the cross and took away my sin and gave me your right life." But the Bible shows us that even this faith (which means believing something) is a

Ephesians 2:8 present from God himself.

We chose Christ because he chose us. We loved him because

1 John 4:19 he loved us. This is great news for us, because we know that if God has chosen us, we can be sure he will not then throw us away

John 6:39 [*assurance*]. He will always keep us and make sure we keep going as Christians [*perseverance*].

So, we are made to live by God when we believe the good news about Jesus. We believe because God has put it into our hearts

Romans 8:30 to believe. It is all down to him. At the same time, God changes us with the change we have already learned about. He takes away our sin and gives us Jesus' right life.

Ephesians 1:5 He also makes us part of his family [*adoption*]. He becomes our Father and we become his sons. The Bible sometimes uses the word "son" to talk about men and women because only sons were important in Bible times. Christian men and Christian women are all sons of the living God when we are saved.

This is a big change. We were dead. Now we are living. We were against God, now we are for him. We were children of the Devil. Now we are children of God. These are all Bible ways to describe what has taken place in us.

Before we could not know God. Now, as Christians, we do know God. Remember we said there are two important questions in life. What is God like? and How can we know God? Now we have answers to these questions. We can know God through Jesus who was killed in our place. There is no greater piece of news that we could receive or believe.

How does God work in us?

Who is the Holy Spirit?

We have learned that God is three-in-one. He is God the Father, God the Son and God the Holy Spirit. The Holy Spirit takes the work that God wants to do and makes it happen. For example, in the first part of the Bible, the Old Testament, the Holy Spirit is **Psalm 33:6** sometimes called the breath of God. The Bible says God uses his breath (the Holy Spirit) to make things.

It is important for us to understand that the Holy Spirit is **2 Cor. 3:3** fully God, just as Jesus is fully God. All the things we learned about God in the first part of this book are true for God the Holy Spirit, just as they are true for the Father and the Son. Because the Holy Spirit is God, we should refer to the Holy Spirit as "he" not as "it". **John 16:13** If we do not do this, we may forget that he is God, just as the Father is God and the Son is God.

The Old Testament looks forward to a time when the Holy **Joel 2:28** Spirit will come to Earth, just as it looks forward to a time when Jesus will come to Earth. In fact, the two are linked. Jesus teaches **John 14:16** that the Holy Spirit, when he comes, will carry on the work that Jesus has started.

Acts 2 The coming of the Holy Spirit is shown in the book of Acts. It took place at a special Jewish time called [*Pentecost*] and so this is what Christians also call this moment in history.

Jesus said the Holy Spirit would come

John 14:16 When Jesus came to Earth he taught his friends that he would not leave them alone, but send the Holy Spirit to be their helper. He said the Holy Spirit would be another helper. He meant that the Holy Spirit would carry on the work that Jesus started.

Jesus said the Holy Spirit would also be different from him. Jesus came to Earth as a man. This meant that he could only be in one place at a time. But Jesus said the Holy Spirit would live in all Christians, wherever they lived. The Bible sometimes calls the Holy Spirit the "Spirit of Jesus." This is a good name for the Holy Spirit because Jesus said that when the Holy Spirit came to live in men and women, it was just like having Jesus living in them.

Acts 16:7

In fact, Jesus taught that the time when the Holy Spirit came would be even better than when Jesus was on Earth. This is because the Holy Spirit came to the Earth after Jesus had been killed and made to live again. Men and women could enjoy what Jesus had done for them when he was killed on the cross. The Holy Spirit is also, as we have just learned, able to be with all Christians. Jesus said that in the time of the Holy Spirit we would see greater things than even those Jesus did.

John 14:12

For example, when the Holy Spirit first came, over three thousand men and women became Christians in one day, something that never took place when Jesus was on the Earth.

Acts 2:41

What does the Holy Spirit do?

The most important thing that the Holy Spirit does is to bring glory to Jesus. It is worth learning about this. Because God existed before all things, he should receive all the praise of everything in the world [*he is worthy*]. That is why, for example, the Bible shows us that all things were made for Jesus.

John 16:14

Colossians 1:16

It is sin not to give God this praise that we should give to him. Sin means that we often put other things first [*idolatry*]. This is what took place when Adam and Eve first turned their backs on God. They put themselves first, rather than putting God first. They did not give God the glory that he should have received.

Exodus 20:4

Genesis 3:6

33

Exodus 20:5 God wants to receive all the glory [we say he is a *jealous God*]. In men and women this would be a wrong thing, but in God it is another part of being right all the time. God should receive the praise from all men and women, and he is right to be angry when he does not receive it.

When the Holy Spirit works in us, he makes sure that glory goes to Jesus, even though we once did not follow him as we should have done. He does this by changing us.

The Holy Spirit brings us to God

Ephesians 2:1-10 In the last part of this book, we learned that the death of Jesus can change us from being dead to being alive. Even though we once turned our back on God, like all men and women, God is able to change us around and make us know him.

John 3:5 The Bible teaches us that it is the Holy Spirit who makes this change. He brings us the new life. He does this by helping us to see **John 16:18** what we are like and how we have turned away from God. He then shows us how we need to turn back to God and makes it possible for us to do so. We learned that when we believed that Jesus took our **Ephesians 2:8** place on the cross, it was because God gave us the present of faith.

Now we can see that this present comes because the Holy Spirit is at work in us. This process often starts when we begin to see how serious sin is and that we, like all men and women are full of sin [*conviction*]. It is also the Holy Spirit who helps us to understand that Jesus is a man and fully God at the same time.

Now we understand that the Spirit works in us to change us, we can say something else about the change God makes. The Spirit **1 Cor. 3:16** comes and lives within all those who become Christians – all those whom God saves. The Bible says we are the house [*temple*] of the **1 Kings 8:11** Holy Spirit. In the Old Testament, the House of God [the *temple*] was the place where God showed himself. Now that the Spirit has come, we do not need a special building. The Spirit comes and makes his house in us. This joins us to Jesus [**union with Christ**]. We are not just friends or brothers of Jesus, but Jesus comes and makes his house in us through his Spirit.

In other religions, men and women follow their gods. In Christianity, God comes and lives in us and is joined to us. This makes Christianity different from other religions.

The Holy Spirit makes us like God

Once we have become Christians we still need to be changed. God's plan for us is for us to be more and more like Jesus. Jesus lived on Earth as the man who was always right. He never did anything wrong and God wants us to be like this as well.

Before we were Christians we were ruled by sin. Sin made us do, say and think things that were not right. Now that the Spirit of Jesus lives in us, we are no longer ruled by sin. But we know that we still do things wrong. Why is this? It is because we are not exactly like Jesus. Sin still has an effect on us, even though it does not rule over us [**indwelling sin**].

Romans 6:2

Galatians 5:17

Once the Spirit has shown us that we need to be saved and has changed our hearts, we still need him. He keeps changing us to be more like Jesus. We should be able to look at our lives and see how God is doing this work. If we cannot see this, it may be because we are stopping the Spirit from this important work. This process of change [**sanctification**] continues right until we die when God does the last work necessary to change us once and for all.

2 Cor. 3:17

As Christians, the Holy Spirit changes what we wish for. Before we were Christians, we wanted things that were good for us. Now we want things that are good for God. Just as the Holy Spirit wants to bring glory to Jesus, so he makes us want the same thing. Glory is given to Jesus as we become more and more like him.

How do we know that we are becoming more like Jesus? We can read the Bible to see what Jesus is like. We can also see if our lives have the fruit that the Spirit brings. The fruit of the Spirit are the things that men and women who have been changed by God show in their lives.

The fruit of the Spirit

Galatians
5:22-26 It is worth learning about the fruit of the Spirit. In the book of Galatians, Paul writes to Christians who are living by keeping laws. These laws were the old Jewish laws. Paul shows them that keeping those old laws is not what is needed. When the Spirit comes to live in us, he overpowers the old heart [*the sinful nature*] so that we do not do what our old self wanted. Instead we live by the Spirit of Jesus.

Galatians
5:19-21 Paul lists the things that go with the old self and the things that go with the Spirit. Those who have been changed by the Spirit of Jesus should have the things that go with the Spirit. If these are not in our lives, we need to ask God to change us and focus on living in a different way.

Of course, all Christians have good days and bad days. Some days we are not very good at being like Jesus. The bad days should make us think about our lives and try, with God's help, to live by the Spirit.

There are nine parts to the fruit of the Spirit. These are not nine different fruits. We need to show them all if we are to be like Jesus. Make sure you understand them all.

John
3:16 ■ Love. Remember that God has loved us. That is why he sent Jesus to die in our place. The Spirit changes us so that we show this love to others. It is a love which puts others first. Matthew
5:44 We must love other Christians, but if we are to be like Jesus,

we must also love those who are against us. We were against God, but he still loved us when he gave us Jesus.

- Joy. The joy of a Christian is more than being happy. Christians can be joyful even when things around them are not happy. In fact, the Bible shows us we must be joyful all the time. Again, Jesus is our example. He had joy even as he went to be killed. Our joy does not come from the things that are taking place around us, but from knowing God even though we once turned our backs on him.

Phil. 4:4

Hebrews 12:2

- Peace. To have peace is to not worry about things. Christians have peace because we know that God is in control of all things, as we have already learned. We also know that the we are God's children and that we will always be his children. We are certain about this [*assurance*] and part of the work of the Holy Spirit is to tell us that our new life in Jesus will never be taken away.

Matthew 6:25-34

Romans 8:16

- Being patient. The Spirit helps us to be patient. We need to be patient with others, and also patient to see everything God says coming true. We do not always see this happen right away. Men and women often get cross when things do not go their way. Christians remain calm because God's Spirit helps us be patient.

Ephesians 4:2

2 Peter 3:9

- Being kind. God has been kind to us, and it should not be possible for us to be unkind to others. We have all met men and women who are unkind, but the Spirit makes Christians different.

Titus 3:4

- Being good. Being good is similar to being kind. Being kind is about what we do. Being good is about what comes from our hearts. These are hearts that the Spirit has changed.

- Being gentle. The Spirit helps us act to others in the same way Jesus acted. He was always gentle. Sometimes he was

Matthew 11:29

37

firm, but even then, he was still gentle. He was not violent.

Matthew 5:39 Christians must not be violent. In fact, Jesus teaches us that if someone attacks us, we must not attack them back. Most men and women would attack back. But the Spirit helps us be different from most men and women.

3 John 3 ■ Being faithful. Being faithful is being true to what we have said. As Christians we must be faithful to God. We have said we will follow him, and we must. But being faithful is also about how we treat others. Christians must be true to their word. If we say we will do something, we must do it. Others must know that we will be like this.

2 Cor. 10:5 ■ Showing self-control. The last part of the fruit of the Spirit is being able to control ourselves. We need this because of the sin that is still in us. This means being able to stop ourselves from doing things we know we should not do and saying wrong things.

You can see that we need to be changed to be like Jesus! This is a good part of the Bible to use as a prayer. It helps us see how much we need the work of the Holy Spirit in us. We cannot live for Jesus by ourselves and without him. It is not possible.

The Holy Spirit fills us

Ephesians 5:18 What we need is for the Holy Spirit to fill us up [This is sometimes called **baptism in the Holy Spirit**]. When we are first saved, the Holy Spirit fills us up. He must do, because this is the only way that those who are dead could be made living again. But as we go through life we sometimes stop the Spirit working in us.

We need to be always asking God to fill us with his Spirit. Some Christians think this only takes place once in your life. However, in the Bible, it seems that we need to be filled every day with the Spirit of Jesus. This is the only way that we will be changed to be like Jesus.

The Holy Spirit helps us to pray

We learned at the start that God loves to talk to us. He also loves us to talk to him. We call this prayer. It is the Holy Spirit who helps us to pray. He gives us the words to say and makes it possible for us to come to God in prayer. We could say that he keeps the lines open. We do not need to pray to the Holy Spirit. He is in us helping us to pray to God the Father or God the Son. But he makes sure our prayers are heard by our Heavenly Father. **Romans 8:26-27**

The Holy Spirit helps us to serve God

You can see that the work God the Holy Spirit does in us is very great indeed. There is something more we need to learn about it. The Bible shows us that the Spirit also helps us to serve God.

When God saves us, he saves us for a purpose. We have already seen how he wants all the glory to come to him. One of the ways that glory comes to him is by his children doing things for him. The Holy Spirit helps us in this service by giving us abilities which we can use [*gifts of the Spirit*].

Some of these abilities are listed in the Bible. This is not a complete list. You will see that some of them are very broad abilities – like showing mercy. Showing mercy could include all kinds of things. It could include being kind, giving money to the poor, helping older men and women and so on. However, these abilities do give us an idea of how God wants us to serve him. You can read about these abilities in three particular places. **Romans 12:1-8**

1 Cor. 12

1 Peter 4:10-11

Notice that these abilities are different in the three letters. The abilities given to Christians at Rome seem to be different from those given to Christians at Corinth and those shown by Peter.

There are some important things to learn about these abilities which Paul shows to the church in Corinth. When you read this part of the Bible you will see that:

1 Cor. 12:7 ■ the abilities are given to build the church

1 Cor. 12:29-30 ■ not everyone is given all the abilities

■ the abilities do not make anyone a special kind of Christian. All Christians are the same before God

Some of the abilities need to be explained because it is not always clear what they are. The abilities listed below are the ones that are hardest to understand and the ones that Christians sometimes cannot agree upon.

1 Cor. 12:10

1 Peter 4:11

■ [*Prophecy*]. In the Old Testament, the prophets showed men and women what God thought and said. In particular, they showed that Jesus would come to Earth and sort out the problem of sin. In the New Testament, Jesus is called The Prophet, the one who brings God's words to Earth. The first New Testament prophets spoke before the Bible was written. They told people what God wanted to say. Now that the Bible is written down, prophets can show people what God wants to say by explaining what is in the Bible. That way we can be sure that we are hearing God's words and not man's words.

1 Cor. 12:10

1 Cor. 12:9

■ [*Healings*] and [*Miracles*]. In Bible times some men and women were given the ability of working miracles – doing things that only God could do. They could also make those who were ill well again. These powers came from God through men and women. If you read through the book of Acts you will see that these abilities were not given very often. Miracles sometimes happen to prove the Bible's message, for example in places where men and women have never heard of Christianity. We should not expect to see them all the time. Satan can also do powerful things, so we must

40

take great care in believing that miracles always come from God. The way the abilities are written about in the Bible makes us think that the abilities were only given for one miracle at a time: so no-one has the right to claim they are a miracle worker.

2 Thess. 2:9

■ [**Tongues**]. It is clear in the book of Acts that God gives some men and women the ability to speak different languages. This is more than learning a new language in school. When this took place in church, it was difficult to understand, so Paul said it should not happen very often and that if someone used another language it should always be interpreted.

Acts 2:1-11

1 Cor. 14:13-19

The other abilities are not so difficult to understand. They include serving, showing mercy, leading and encouraging. What we must see is that whatever work God gives us to do, he also gives us the ability to do it, through the power of the Holy Spirit.

The Holy Spirit brings us together

We have started to see one last important work of the Holy Spirit. When he gives abilities to Christians it is for the "common good". The Holy Spirit works to bring Christians together [**unity**] as a group, called the church. This is so important that we shall learn about it in another part of the book.

Ephesians 4:3

The Holy Spirit made men write the Bible

One of the most important jobs the Holy Spirit has done is to help men write the Bible. Because the Holy Spirit helped these men, we know that the Bible comes from God. This is the subject for our next part of this book.

2 Peter 1:21

41

How does God speak to us?

Right at the start we said 'How do we know what God is like?' Men and women have very different ideas about what God is like. They all think they are right. How do we know what Christians believe is the right thing to believe? Remember that God is completely different from us. We cannot simply look at others or plants or flowers and say 'Yes, I know exactly what God is like.' If God is

Hebrews 1:1-2 different from us, the only way we will be able to know what he is like is if he shows us himself. We call this [*revelation*]. We mean that God shows himself to us.

How does he do this? He does it in two ways. First he shows us something about himself through what he has made. Remember that we said that God made all things. So when we look at the

Romans 1:20 things God has made, they show us something about him. They can show us that he is powerful. Look at the mountains! God made these. It needs great power to make mountains. They can also show us how wise God is. Look at the flowers! Look at the way they grow and how beautiful they are! God must be wise to make such things. When we look at what God has made we can also see that God is real. Some men and women claim that there is no God. When we look around us at the things God has made we can see that this is not true. We call all of this [*general revelation*]. It just shows us general things about God.

But we need to know more than this. The things God has made do not tell us that much about God. They do not tell us how we can know God. They do not tell us about Jesus or the Holy Spirit or that God is our Father. There is so much more we need to know.

John 1:18 God shows himself to us in more detail. We call this [*special*

John 14:9 *revelation*]. Most of all he does that through his Son, the Lord Jesus Christ. Jesus himself said that anyone who had seen him had also seen the Father. Because the Son, the Holy Spirit and the

Father are all one, if we know what the Son is like, we know what the Father and the Spirit are like, and so on. But how do we know what Jesus is like? He lived 2,000 years past. We cannot see pictures of him. We cannot hear his voice like we can hear other voices which speak out loud.

The Bible is God's Word

This is where we come to the Bible. The Bible is the book that comes from God. We sometimes call it God's Word, as Jesus did. Because it is God's Word the Bible has authority. Men and women think that God shows himself in many other ways. But none of these ways has authority. For example, some men and women think that God speaks to them with a voice in their head. But how do they know where this voice comes from? It may come from God or it may come from their own heart. Others think that God shows himself through what a church leader says. But how do we know the church leader is showing us the truth unless we have some way of checking it?

Mark 7:13

Because the Bible is written down, we can be sure of what we read in it. It is very good that God has shown himself to us in this way. How else could we know what he is like and know how to come to him? All we have seen so far in this book has come from the Bible. That is why we have written the Bible verses at the side of the page. That is also why we want you to look up these verses to make sure what we are showing you is right and that we have not invented it ourselves.

How do know we the Bible is God's Word?

How do we know that this is true? How do we know that the Bible is truly God's Word? Let us consider the two parts of the Bible one at a time. The first part of the Bible is called the [*Old Testament*].

43

This covers the time from when God made the world to a few hundred years before Jesus came into the world. The second part of the Bible is called the [**New Testament**]. This shows us all about Jesus, his death and coming to life again. We also see how the early church spread around the world and what the church believed and taught.

Mark 7:13

When Jesus, the Son of God came to earth, the Old Testament was already in place. Jesus himself called the Old Testament the 'Word of God' and showed how it came from God himself. He believed that the Old Testament was true and that the things that are shown there did happen as they are written. He taught from the Old Testament and used the writings in the Old

Luke 4:14-21

Testament to show who he was. This is why we can be sure that the Old Testament is the Word of God. There are other books written at the same time as the Old Testament that some men and women want to include in the Bible, but we should use the books that Jesus himself used and called 'the Word of God.' These books are listed below.

Exodus	2 Samuel	Job	Ezekiel	Nahum
Leviticus	1 Kings	Psalms	Daniel	Habakkuk
Numbers	2 Kings	Proverbs	Hosea	Zephaniah
Deuteronomy	1 Chronicles	Ecclesiastes	Joel	Haggai
Joshua	2 Chronicles	Song of songs	Amos	Zechariah
Judges	Ezra	Isaiah	Obadiah	Malachi
Ruth	Nehemiah	Jeremiah	Jonah	
1 Samuel	Esther	Lamentations	Micah	

These books are of different kinds. Some books tell the story of what took place. We call these [**narrative**] or [**history**]. Other books contain laws that men and women had to follow. Others are books of poems and songs. Others are books which show the men and women how they should live and that Jesus was soon coming to earth. We call these last books [*prophets*].

What about the New Testament?

The four accounts of Jesus' life are called [*gospels*]. Jesus himself believed in the power and authority of his words and life and we should as well. Jesus chose special men to be his followers and take the news about him through the whole world. He called these followers [*apostles*]. He gave them the power to remember things about himself and write them down. They were also helped by God to teach the early church and the church is built upon the teaching of the Old Testament and the teaching of these apostles.

John 14:25-26

John 16:12-15

Ephesians 2:20

One of the apostles, Peter, calls the writings of another apostle Paul, the Scriptures. This is a word that shows that the New Testament is the Word of God as well as the Old Testament. The books of the New Testament are of two kinds. There are accounts of what took place, just like the Old Testament. There are the four gospels. Acts shows us how the church grew. Then there are letters written by the apostles to churches which show us how to live and what we should believe about God. The books of the New Testament are shown below.

2 Peter 3:15-16

Matthew	1 Corinthians	1 Thessalonians	Hebrews	3 John
Mark	2 Corinthians	2 Thessalonians	James	Jude
Luke	Galatians	1 Timothy	1 Peter	Revelation
John	Ephesians	2 Timothy	2 Peter	
Acts	Philippians	Titus	1 John	
Romans	Colossians	Philemon	2 John	

We need the Bible

Why did God make men write down the Bible? It is because we need the Bible to understand what God is like. We cannot do

Matthew 4:4

without it. How else could we know God? We call this the [*necessity of the Bible*] and it is why Christians love the Bible. What does the Bible show us that we need? It shows us what God is like and how we can know him. It also shows us how he wants us to live. The Bible also shows us about Jesus and the church.

This is why it is so important for Christians to read and know the Bible. Even when Christians cannot read, it is good for them to learn parts of the Bible, for example if someone else can read it to them. It is why we teach the Bible in churches. This is the way God speaks to us – through understanding the words he has caused men to write down.

How did the Bible get written?

In order to understand the Bible well, we need to know how it was written down. These books were all written by men. Often they begin with a title which shows who wrote the book and when. How do we know that these written words are God's Word? Some think that God showed these men exactly what to write, like a manager would tell a secretary what to write in a letter. But this cannot be true. The books of the Bible are all different. The writers bring their own experiences and life to bear on what they write. This is **2 Timothy 3:16** important as it makes the books real for us. God says that he "breathed out" the words of the Bible and this his Spirit "carried" the **2 Peter 1:21** writers along. In other words, we say that the Bible is [*inspired*] by God. This gives the words authority but makes sure we can understand what we read. If the words came directly from God we would find it difficult to understand because God is so different from us. We should be very happy that God chose to speak to us through these men.

The Bible is true

We know the Bible is true because it is God's Word. God's Spirit helped the men write down the words that we have. God does not make errors and he helped the men to write without errors as well. But we have to remember that these men wrote in different languages. They wrote the Old Testament in two languages called Hebrew and Aramaic. They wrote the New Testament in a language called Greek. Before books could be made, the Bible was written out by hand. Whenever men and women copy out some writing they can sometimes make errors. Of course, because they were copying out the Bible they took great care. We can say that the very first time the Bible was written down it was completely without error. As the Bible has been copied, there may be some very small errors (for example a name or a number which is not written down exactly) but these do not change the fact that the Bible is true.

The truth of the Bible is very important for Christians. We can be sure what we read is God's Word. We can be sure that what it teaches us about God is true as the Bible came from God and God does not lie. We can be sure that what we read about ourselves and the future is also true. We can be sure that when we tell others what is in the Bible we are showing them the truth. Christians call this [*inerrancy*]. The Bible is without error.

Titus 1:2

When we read the Bible, however, we must remember that the Bible is written down by men. For example, the Bible speaks about the sun coming up and going down. From science we know that this is not true. It is the earth moving that makes it seem like the sun comes and moves across the sky. But because the Bible was written from the point of view of men this does not change the fact that the Bible is true. It explains things from one point of view. In particular, the poems in the Bible and the words of the prophets often contain picture language. For example, when the prophets

Psalm 50:1

47

Psalm 77:15 speak about the 'mighty arm of God' this does not mean that God has arms and legs. We have already seen that God is spirit. He cannot have arms and legs. The prophets are using the language of the world and things that we understand to describe God who is **John 4:24** beyond our understanding.

The Bible has authority

What should Christians think about the authority of the Bible? Those who do not agree with the authority of the Bible don't like what it says. That is why they do not agree with it. Others like some parts of the Bible, but not all of it. Christians must believe all the Bible.

Because the Bible comes from God we must do what the Bible **2 Timothy 3:16-17** teaches. If the Bible teaches us not to kill, for example, we must be very careful not to kill. If the Bible teaches us to love our enemies, **Matthew 5-7** we must be careful to do that as well. The Bible is the main place from where we get our authority. Even the leaders of churches do not have authority themselves. The only authority they have is the authority that comes from the Word of God. For example, if a church leader tells us to do something that the Bible says is wrong, we must follow the Bible and not the church leader. We must check everything we hear and read against what we read in the Bible to **Acts 17:11** make sure it is true.

To say that we do not believe the Bible is to say that we do **1 John 5:9-10** not believe God.

The Bible is clear

Even the apostles say that there are some parts of the Bible that are **2 Peter 3:16** difficult to understand. Anyone who has ever read the Bible knows that there are some parts that are clear and others parts which seem more difficult. Does this mean that anyone who wants to read the

Bible must go to school and University before they can understand God's word?

The answer is no. Christians believe that the Bible is written in such a way that the things we need to be made right with God and live for him are very clear indeed. We call this the [*clarity*] of Scripture. Of course, it does not mean that every single thing in the Bible is easy to understand. The Bible comes from God and God is different from us. When we try to understand what God is like it will always be beyond our understanding! For example, the Trinity (God the Three-in-One) is very difficult to understand.

2 Timothy 3:15

For many years, the church taught that men and women like us could not understand the Bible. We needed someone to explain it to us. They did not allow men and women like us to own a Bible as they said it was too difficult for us. Now we say that this is not true. We can all read the Bible and we should all read the Bible. We can all understand from it how to know God and live for him. Other men and women can help us understand the hard parts of the Bible, but we can all read and understand the Bible for ourselves.

The Bible is all we need

Christians believe that the Bible has all the teaching that God wants us to receive. If God wants to tell us something about himself, we will find it in the Bible. If we need to know something about ourselves, we will find it in the Bible. If there is something that is not important for us to know, we will not find it. Christians call this the [*sufficiency*] of the Bible.

2 Timothy 3:17

It is why we place such importance on the teaching of the Bible. In it, God has shown us everything we need to know. The Bible itself says that it shows us everything we need to know God and to live a godly life. Of course, the Bible does not tell us everything. It does not tell us everything about God. It could not,

2 Peter 1:3

for God has no start and no end. He is different from us and it would not be possible to describe what God is like using words. So there are some things that God shows us about himself in the Bible. But there are other things that we cannot understand.

Revelation 22:18-19 We must be very careful if we meet men and women who want to add to what God has said in the Bible. Sometimes they will say things like 'God has shown me that...' and then they add something to what the Bible says. Other men and women do something different. They take away something written in the Bible. Adding to the Bible or taking away from it is a very serious thing. God himself says we should not do it, because he has made sure the Bible is right for us and has everything we need.

We may think that the Bible does not help us understand some things that take place us around us now. We think it was written 2,000 years past and it cannot still be true. But God made sure that what was written in the Bible is still true today. We sometimes need to think about how we take the teaching of the Bible and match it to what we see in the world [Christians call this **application**] but God's Word will always be up to date.

We need to be very careful of those who say they have their own message from God. God speaks through the Bible and anybody who speaks what is not in the Bible is not from God.

What is the Bible about?

It is important for us to know what the Bible is about. Some men and women think the Bible is about them. They use the Bible like a book which shows how a motorbike works, or how to mend a bicycle. They only open the Bible when something in their life is not going right. They look for help and nothing else.

Because the Bible is God's word it does give us help when things are difficult. But this is not its main purpose. Its main purpose is to teach us about God. For example, Jesus says that all the Scriptures are about him. In some way they all point to him and show us what he is like. This is a good thing.

John
5:39

The word is not only about men and women. It is about God – the Three-in-One. When we are reading the Bible, this is always the place to start. The Old Testament shows us the need for Jesus to come and save the world. The New Testament shows us that Jesus did come, and what it now means to live as his followers.

Sadly, when we read the Bible, the first thing we think about is ourselves. It is always better to think about God first. Here are a list of questions you could ask when reading the Bible. They are in the right order.

(1) What does this part of the Bible tell me about God: Father, Son and Holy Spirit? What does it show me about what he is like and what he does? This should make me praise God with all my heart.

(2) What does this part of the Bible tell me about God's plan to save the world? Does it show me how much we need God? Does it show me something about how Jesus came into the world to save men and women?

(3) What does this part of the Bible tell me about the church – God's family? We are going to learn more about the church in the next part of the book.

(4) What does this part of the Bible tell me about me? If we ask this question last we are more likely to get the true meaning of the part of God's Word that we are reading. How is God calling me to live as a Christian? What do I need to do differently to live for him? What do I need to change?

Romans 11:33-36   God's Word is very rich. Even if we spend our whole life reading it, we will keep seeing new things to learn and understand. This is because God is completely different from us. We are always learning about him.

What does God want us to do?

If we know what God is like and have found the way to know him through Jesus Christ his Son, we must now ask the question, 'What does God want us to do?' To understand the answer to this question, we need to understand what God teaches us about the church. All the way through the Bible God is interested in men and women together, not just as individuals. Even when the Bible stories are about individuals, they are nearly always part of a group or nation. For example, consider one of the great Bible men, Abraham. God tells Abraham that he will be the father of a new nation. God is interested in the nation. **Genesis 12:2**

Or consider Moses. He was another great Bible man. Yet he was also leader of the nation that God told Abraham about. King David was King of the same nation. **Exodus 19:5-6**

This idea continues into the New Testament. We have seen how it is possible and good for us to know God through Jesus Christ, God's Son. God makes it possible for us to know him so we can be made into a new group of men and women, a group the Bible calls the church. The word church simple means a gathering.

Once we understand this important fact, we can understand what God wants for us. He does not want us to be on our own. In fact, it is not possible to be a Christian on your own. We are always joined with other Christians. We sometimes talk about the church to mean all Christians around the world who have ever lived and ever will [*the Universal Church*]. This is the way the New Testament sometimes uses the word. **Ephesians 5:25**

However, most of the time, the New Testament uses the word church to describe a group of Christians who meet together in one place [*the local Church*]. In the book of Acts, Paul and Peter went on journeys to start new churches, not just to tell men and women about Jesus. They knew that the church was important. **Galatians 1:2** **Acts 14:23**

53

We need to see that the church is not a building, it is the men and women who have believed in Jesus as their Saviour. A church sometimes has a building to meet in, but it does not need one. It can meet under a tree in a village, or in a hall that has been rented. What is important are the men and women.

Why is the church important?

Ephesians 4:16 Why is the church so important? The church is one way that God makes it possible for us to grow and to know more about him. He gives us one another to support, encourage, care and teach. This is why every member in a church is important. We all have a part to play in helping others. This is a very good way of building one another up. For example, when someone is sad, others can provide comfort. At the same time, there may be someone who is happy, and we can all share these things together.

There may be someone who is poor and someone else who has more. Sharing our things in this way makes sure that no one loses out. Some in the church may be better at understanding the Bible. They can teach us. And so on. The importance of the church is shown in the words that are used to describe it. Although the word 'church' is used most often, there are other words God uses in the Bible to describe the church.

The people of God

1 Peter 2:9 In the Old Testament, the people of God were one nation, Israel. God looked after them, gave them laws to follow and leaders to govern them. The nation of Israel is a picture of the church. In the New Testament it becomes clear that the people of God are now those who have believed and trusted in the Lord Jesus Christ. The church is now the people of God. God cares for them, gives them laws to follow and leaders to govern them, just as he did for Israel.

He also makes promises to the church about the future. Many of the New Testatment writers use these words to describe the church.

We may feel we belong to a particular nation, for example India. But the Bible says that once we believe and know God we are strangers and foreigners to the world and we belong to a new people – the people of God, which is the church. This is always where our first love is. So we can still love the country in which we are born, but we must love the church more. That is what is important to God, and it must be important to us as well.

1 Peter 2:11

The family of God

The same idea is shown in another word that God uses to describe the church. He calls it the family of God. A family is a place where every member has a relationship to the other. In fact, Christians are brothers and sisters to one another, and these are words we often use to address one another. In a family, relations are very strong. Even when brothers or sisters do something to wrong us we can quickly forgive them because they are part of our family. It is the same with the family of God.

Ephesians 3:15

Jesus himself said that he would come to make families come apart. He meant that some in one family would believe in him and others would not. But even when our own families do not want to know us any more because we have believed in Jesus, we have a new family which we can be part of.

Matthew 10:35

The body of Christ

The apostle Paul uses another word to describe the church – he calls the church the body of Christ. Sometimes Paul talks about Jesus being the body, and all the Christians being members of the one body. Other times, he speaks in a different way, with Christ being the head of the body.

1 Cor. 12:27

1 Cor.
12:12-31
The body of Christ is a very helpful picture. Paul uses it to explain how things should work in the church. Not every part of a body is exactly the same. The foot is not the same as a hand. Every part of a body has a different thing to do. But all the parts of the body are important. None is more important than others. Paul explains this very clearly. Some men and women in the church have things to do that the world thinks very important. But the truth is that every part in the church is important, and we must take care to value every member who is in the church.

The temple of the Holy Spirit

In the Old Testament, the people of God built a temple. Although God cannot be put into a building, this was the place that he showed himself to his people. When Jesus came, he said that we did not need a temple, because he was the temple. We have already seen that if we want to know what God the Father is like, we need to look at his Son, Jesus Christ. Jesus is the one who shows the Father to us.

But now Jesus has gone into heaven, the Bible teaches us that the church is God's temple. We have already seen that God lives in every one of us through his Holy Spirit. But he comes and lives in the church in a special way. Jesus teaches that when men and women meet together, Jesus comes to them. Of course, Jesus is with us all the time, but this means that the church together is more special than individual Christians.

The flock of the Shepherd

Jesus says that he is the Good Shepherd. He shows us that we are his sheep, part of his flock. This is a good picture of the church because sheep need looking after. They cannot look after themselves. They need a shepherd to care for them and feed them. The Bible calls the leaders in churches under-shepherds. They serve the flock which belongs to the Great Shepherd, Jesus. This means that churches do not belong to leaders – Jesus is head of the church.

1 Peter 5:2-4

The bride of Christ

There is one last picture of the church that we need to know about. It is especially used when the Bible shows what will happen to the church in the future. We will think about the future in another part of this book, but we need to understand that God has a great plan for the future. That plan is to make all things new and perfect. The world will be made new again and Christians will be able to leave sin behind once and for all.

This will all happen when Jesus returns. His return is like the coming of the bridegroom to a wedding. Who is the bride? The Bible tells us the bride is the church. She will be dressed in white robes, which is a picture of purity and being without sin. She will be with Jesus for evermore in the new world which he is making. This is the purpose of the church in the future.

Matthew 25:1-13

Revelation 21:9-10

What does the church do now?

We now know what the church is going to be like in the future. But what should the church be like now? Much of the teaching of the New Testament explains this. It shows us what men and women who have been changed by God should be like. It shows us how we should live. It shows us how we should relate to one another and care for one another.

The first church started in Jerusalem at a time we call Pentecost when the Holy Spirit came to earth in power. Peter spoke about Jesus and 3,000 men and women believed what he said. Then we read what the first church did. This is an important part of the Bible as it shows us what the church should be doing as we wait for the return of Jesus. There are five parts to it.

Acts 2:14-41

Acts 2:42-47

Teaching

The early church gave themselves to learning about Jesus and what it means to follow him. At first they had the apostles to teach them these things. Now we have them written down in the Bible. This is what churches do. When the Christians meet together someone teaches and explains the Bible so that we know more about God. We call this teaching [*preaching*].

1 Peter 4:11
Speaking in this way is one of the gifts of the Spirit that we saw in the last chapter. God gives this gift to some in the church so that all in the church can grow. But the Bible also tells us that we

Colossians 3:16
have to teach one another. We do this by talking with one another all the time about things we are learning about God in his Word. This means that the learning times in church are not just when someone speaks from the front, but any moment that we spend together talking about the Word of God.

Fellowship

The first church also gave themselves to fellowship. This is a word that means being together and helping one another. It can take

Acts 4:32-35
many forms, but in Acts we see it means practical as well as spiritual care. Those with more care for those with less. But fellowship is more than being together. It is also sharing the same purpose, thinking the same about issues, wanting the same things. We sometimes call this [*unity*]. Unity is a form of fellowship, and the New Testament writers are careful to teach it. Often churches lack unity. This is because men and women are most interested in themselves, not in others. In a church which is giving themselves to fellowship, men and women think of others before themselves and

Phil. 2:1-4
this helps everyone to get along. We should enjoy being with each other more than we even enjoy being with our earthly families.

Worship

The early church met together and broke bread. This is what we call worship. Worship is where Christians meet together and give praise to God, most often by singing his praises. The Bible is clear that singing Christian songs is an important part of church life.

Colossians 3:16

The breaking of bread service [also called **The Lord's Supper** or, sometimes, **Communion**] is a particular way of worshipping Jesus taught to us by Jesus himself. It comes from the meal he shared with his followers the night before he was killed. He took bread, broke it, and shared it with his friends. He told them that the bread was to help them remember his body which was broken on the cross. Then he took wine and shared it with his friends. He told them that the wine was to help them remember his blood which left his body for them. This is a meal the church continues to have to remember Jesus and his death. It helps us remember that Jesus, the Son of God, had to die in our place, and fills us with praise.

1 Cor. 11:17-34

It is not a magical meal. The bread is not actually Jesus body. The wine is not actually Jesus blood. They are signs of the real thing to help us remember. All churches celebrate the Lord's Supper. Some churches do this every week, some every month. It does not matter how often we take this meal, as long as we do it enough to help us remember.

Prayer

The first church also prayed together. Prayer is talking to God. Every Christian has the ability to talk to God and should talk to God. But we can also come to God as Christians together in the church. Normally one person prays at a time so the others can hear what is being said. Then everybody else can join with a word at the end – normally this word is 'Amen' which is a sign of agreement. In this way the prayer becomes the prayer of the whole church.

Psalm 139:4 God likes to hear our prayers. We do not know why this is, because he knows what we are going to say even before we say it. But when we pray, we show to others and to him that we believe in him and that we need his help. In the book of Acts, great things **Acts 4:31** happen when men and women pray.

Witness

There is one last thing that a church should do. It should tell others about Jesus and the cross. We call this [*witness*] or [*evangelism*]. When Jesus was on earth, some of the last words he gave to his friends were commands to go and tell others about him. In the book of Acts we see men and women going all around the world to tell others about God.

Acts 2:47 This must have taken place in the first church because we see that every day God made more men and women Christians. This is because the church was telling others about him and how they could know him.

Every church must do these five things. They must be interested in the teaching of the Bible and meet together to learn. They must enjoy being together and helping one another. They must worship God and pray to him, and make sure they find ways to tell others about Jesus and the cross.

Becoming part of a church

How do you become part of a church? The Bible teaches us that we must be born again to be part of a church. We must have believed **1 Cor. 15:3-4** that Jesus is God and has been killed for our sins on the cross, then come back from the dead. These are the most important things for us to believe. When we turn to Jesus, we put our old life away and start again. Christians show this by being [*baptised*]. The church Matthew 28:19 baptises men and women who have believed in Jesus. Baptism is when we go down into water, go right under the water, then come out again. Jesus himself was baptised. Baptism shows us many things.

It shows us that our sins are taken away. Baptism does not itself take away our sins but it is a sign that Jesus has done this for us.

Baptism also shows that our new life has started. Going into Romans 6:1-4 the water is like going into a grave. Coming out from the water is like coming back from the dead.

We only need to be baptised once to show others what has taken place. It should be something that takes place so the whole church can see how we have been changed. They will praise God with us that the church has grown by one person!

Sometimes men and women become Christians in very hot countries where there is no water to be baptised in. This does not matter. Instead, we can put a little water over someone. It is still a good sign and it still shows the change that has taken place. What is important is that this takes place after we have believed. It is a sign of what has already taken place in our lives.

We are now ready to be part of the church!

Leaders in the church

It helps the church to have leaders. These are men who help direct 1 Timothy 3:1-13 the work of the church, in particular the teaching that needs to happen [we call them *elders*]. There are important rules for Titus 1:6-9 leaders which are set out in the Bible. You can read the part of the Bible to see what it says. In particular leaders must be men. Some think this is because women do not matter to God. This is not so. 1 Timothy 2:12 Before God every man and woman is equal. In fact, in the church,

God breaks down every division that we make and makes us all one. These include divisions between men and women, between different kinds of workers, different languages and different cultures. None of these matter in church.

So why do leaders of churches have to be men? It is because God has made an order in the world. This comes in the very first book of the Bible when God makes man first, then makes woman. This does not mean that man is more important than woman, just that he has different things in mind for them. Christians do not get their importance from what they do, like others in the world. Our importance comes from knowing God.

The future of the church

We have already seen the future that God has for the church. The church should always be thinking about this and becoming ready for the time when Jesus will come again. This means becoming more and more like Jesus. Jesus is perfect and his church should be perfect too. Remember, we call this difference [*holiness*]. We should grow as Christians. This means Christians in the church should be more like Jesus every day and know more about him every

day. We call this process [*sanctification*].

The more we become like Jesus, the more we see how much more we have to change! This process lasts our whole life. The church is a great place to grow to be more like Jesus. Others can help us and show us where we are going wrong. We can help others. This is all part of the fellowship we saw earlier. Together we grow to be like Jesus as we wait for his return.

The life of the church

It is not surprising that the world views the church the same way it

viewed Jesus Christ. This is part of being like him. Therefore life can be difficult for the church and its members. There are men and women who don't like what we teach, just as they did not like what Jesus taught. Some men and women just walk away from the church's teaching. Others want to do bad things to Christians to stop them teaching. This took place right from the start when Jewish leaders tried to stop Peter and John from teaching about Jesus. They would not agree to it. **Acts 4:20**

From then it has been hard being a Christian. We can even face death for our faith. But we must keep going. The Bible tells us to expect this reaction. We call it [*persecution*] or [*suffering*]. There are many good things that the Bible says to men and women who suffer in this way. We must expect this kind of attack and praise God that others are doing to us what they did to Jesus. But we must never fight back, because God calls us to be different from the world. This can be very hard, but we must pray to God to help us stay calm. God promises he will always give us the strength to keep going when we suffer. **Acts 14:22** **1 Peter 2:21** **2 Cor. 12:9**

What will God do in the future?

So far, all the things we have thought about are things God has done in the past or is doing in the present. The Bible, God's Word, shows us all about these things, but also shows us what God will do in the future. We can be sure that God will do all the things he says he will do, because he has already started to keep his word. For example, he said he would send a Saviour to the world, and he did this when he sent his own Son, Jesus Christ.

Men and women want to know what will happen in the future. Christians don't need to worry about this because God himself shows us clearly what will happen.

Death

The Bible links sin to death. In the good garden that God made, death was part of the punishment for not keeping God's commands.

Genesis 2:17 Because all men and women sin, they also all die. We have all seen this around us. Men and women get sick, grow old, have accidents

Hebrews 9:27 and everyone dies. The Bible says this will happen to all of us.

But death is not the end. It cannot be the end because God has made us to live forever. How then, when our bodies are getting weaker and weaker can we live forever. To understand this we have to see that our lives are made up of two parts. We have bodies and we have a spirit [sometimes called a *soul*]. The body we are in gets old and grows weak because of the effect of sin in the world. It does not matter if we are a Christian or not, this will still happen.

2 Cor. 4:16 We shall see in a moment that we will be given new bodies. But for now, we need to understand that our bodies waste away and die but the the spiritual part of us – our soul – will always live on. The question we must ask is, what will happen to it after I die?

Heaven

The Bible teaches us that there are just two places where we can go after we die. One, the place where God lives, is called heaven. This is a perfect place. In heaven there is no illness, no crying and no death. There God's church will give praise to him – Father, Son and Holy Spirit, for ever and ever. It is not possible to imagine what this will be like. The Bible uses beautiful pictures to describe it. These pictures are probably not what it is like, but images that help us understand what a beautiful place it will be. The souls of Christians who die go straight away to heaven. We know this because Jesus said it to a man who was killed at the same time as Jesus.

Revelation 21:4

Revelation 21

Luke 23:43

The only reason we can get to heaven is because Jesus makes it possible. Remember that we said that God takes away our sins and gives us Jesus' right life. When we get to heaven, God will accept us because he sees Jesus' right life.

This means that Jesus is the only way to heaven. Jesus himself said this. If there was another way to heaven, then it would not have been necessary for Jesus to come and die. God would have found another way. But because Jesus was sent by his Father, we know this is the only way to heaven.

John 14:6

Hell

There is another place that the souls of men and women can go when they die. This is called Hell. Jesus taught his friends about this place. It is a very bad place of punishment. Like heaven it goes on for ever. Sin is so serious that men and women who have not had Jesus' right life given to them, must pay the punishment. We also should go to hell – this is what God has saved us from.

Luke 16:19-31

It is hard to imagine how bad this place will be. No one should want to go there. We should not want anyone else to go there, and it is one of the reasons we should want to tell others

65

about how God has made it possible to go to heaven rather than go to hell.

2 Peter 2:4 The Bible shows us that Satan and the other bad angels called demons will all be punished in hell alongside others who have not turned to Jesus.

Hope

When we think about hell it makes some Christians worry. What if I die and find out that I am going to hell after all? We don't need to worry like this, because God gives us hope. Christian hope is certain about the future. Because God has saved us (we did not save ourselves) we can be sure that God will keep us and make sure we go to heaven. We call this hope [**assurance**]. It is part of the work of the Holy Spirit to show to us that we are God's children and we will not have to go to hell.

What about those who have not heard about Jesus? At this point, some Christians worry about what will happen to others. As we have already said, when we think about heaven and hell it should make us want to tell others about the good news of Jesus. But what about those who have never heard about Jesus? We cannot say what will happen to others.

God does not punish people for not hearing the gospel but for sinning against him. It is not for us to decide how God will judge those who do not know about him. But we can be sure that God the Judge will do the right thing.

Genesis 18:25

However, we do know that men and women can go to heaven only through Jesus. It may be that God will always find a way to tell others about Jesus – but we must use this thought to make us go out into the whole world. If we hear about places where men and women don't know Jesus, the church must go there and tell them!

We do know that God is just and fair. We can be sure that when it comes to the death of men and women God will always do the right thing.

The second coming

All of this sounds great news! Life in heaven is going to be so much better than life on earth. Imagine a life with no illness and no sin! We should all look forward to this time. In fact, the Bible shows us that heaven is our real house. It is where we should be. We should feel like we are in another country when we live on the earth. We do not belong. Instead we belong to the kingdom of heaven. So, Christians must never worry about death because death, though it is sad for those we leave, takes us to the place where we want to be.

Phil. 1:21

1 Peter 2:11

However, there is more to life after death than this. The Bible shows us that God wants to do something bigger. He wants to make all things new. He will do this by starting again – by making a new earth and a new heaven where all his children can live. To mark this moment, he will send his Son to the earth again – we call this the Second Coming.

Revelation 21:1

When will Jesus return?

The first question that always comes into our minds is when will this happen? The Bible shows us that no one knows the answer to this question. It could happen at any moment, or it could take thousands of years. If God had shown us the answer, then it would change the way we live. We would live however we liked until the time of Jesus' return, then we would change.

Luke 24:36

This is not the way God wants us to live. Because we do not know the time, we should always be ready for the return of Jesus. The Bible says this makes us watch and pray. It should change how we live every moment of every day.

Luke 21:36

It also means that we must be quick to tell others about Jesus, because we might soon run out of time.

What will happen?

Christians are always interested in what will happen when Jesus comes back. However, the Bible gives us very few details. It is not worth worrying about all the details. We will find out when it takes place! Let us consider the things the Bible does tell us.

Revelation 1:7 God shows us that everyone will know when Jesus comes back. If someone says to you that it has already taken place, they are not saying the truth, because when Jesus returns every eye will see him.

Phil. 2:10 At that moment, everybody will give praise to Jesus. This does not mean that they will go to heaven, but they will see that Jesus is real and that he is the Son of God. But once Jesus returns it will be too late to turn to him. Men and women must do that before he returns.

1 Cor. 15:49 At the return of Jesus, all men and women will be given new bodies. Our spirits will be joined again with new perfect bodies like the one Jesus had when he came back to life. It does not matter if we have believed in Jesus or not. Then we will be ready for God to act as judge. We call this the [*Day of Judgement*].

The Day of Judgement

Hebrews 9:27-28 In the Bible, God is often called the Judge. He always acts as a Judge, but we see this clearly on the Day of Judgement. There men and women must give an account of themselves before him. We have already seen that the only way to be "not guilty" is to have believed in Jesus to take away our sins and give us his right life.

Christians need not worry about the Day of Judgement. We already know what the Judge will say – he will say we are not guilty

68

and allow our new bodies to live in his new heavens and earth that he has made. The judgement for Christians is to see how we have used the gifts that God has given us and how we have loved him. We will receive a reward for our service. We do not know what kind of reward this will be. We also know that we will not be looking at the rewards of others and thinking 'I wish I had that reward' because that will be sin and there is no sin in the new heavens and earth.

But the idea of rewards should make us serve the Lord with all our heart now so that God is pleased with us on the Day of Judgement. **Ephesians 6:8**

For those who have not believed in Jesus, the Day of Judgement will be the day when God sends men and women to hell. For them, it is a very bad day indeed, and they will suffer for ever and ever.

The New Heaven and Earth

We will spend eternal life (life for ever and ever) in the new heaven and earth. It will never come to an end and we will never lose our joy. There we will go on knowing God and growing in how much we know him. Even though we live forever we are still limited and so there will always be something more to know about God. What a life this will be!

As we think about the new heaven and earth, we should look forward to it. It is so much better than this life that we should want it to come as soon as possible. The very last parts of the Bible express this wish. "Amen. Come, Lord Jesus." **Revelation 22:20**

Index of difficult words